Mini Desserts

Mini Desserts

LOVE
FOOD™

This edition published in 2013

LOVE FOOD is an imprint of Parragon Books Ltd

Parragon
Chartist House
15–17 Trim Street
Bath BA1 1HA, UK

Copyright © Parragon Books Ltd 2012

LOVE FOOD and the accompanying heart device is a registered trademark of Parragon Books Ltd in
Australia, the UK, India, and the EU.

www.parragon.com/lovefood

ISBN: 978-1-4723-1653-0

Printed in China

Created and produced by Pene Parker and Becca Spry
Author and home economist: Sara Lewis
Photographer: William Shaw

Notes for the reader

This book uses standard kitchen measuring spoons and cups. All spoon and cup measurements
are level unless otherwise indicated. Unless otherwise stated, milk is assumed to be whole, butter is
assumed to be salted, eggs are large, and individual fruits are medium.

The times given are only an approximate guide. Preparation times differ according to the techniques
used by different people and the cooking times may also vary from those given. Optional ingredients,
variations, or serving suggestions have not been included in the calculations.

Recipes using raw or very lightly cooked eggs should be avoided by infants, the elderly, pregnant
women, and people with weakened immune systems. Pregnant and breast-feeding women are
advised to avoid eating peanuts and peanut products. People with nut allergies should be aware that
some of the prepared ingredients used in the recipes in this book may contain nuts. Always check the
packaging before use.

Contents

Introduction

Impress your friends at your next dinner party, birthday celebration, or other special occasion with these dainty mini desserts. If you want the option of serving a tiny sweet treat or, for a smart restaurant feel, two or three different desserts on one plate per person, instead of a whole dessert, then these recipes are for you. For an informal gathering, arrange these baby desserts on large plates or trays, much like canapés, and pass them around.

Equipment

Pans and molds

You may have some dishes already, perhaps liqueur glasses, a mini muffin pan, ovenproof ramekins (individual ceramic dishes), or demitasse coffee cups. Additional dishes can be bought from kitchen shops, the chinaware section of a department store, or online. Plastic shot glasses are available from supermarkets.

The dishes used are between ¼ cup and ⅓ cup in volume. Where small silicone muffin cups are used, a measurement has been given for the bottom of the muffin cups; metal mini muffin pans with 12 or 24 cups are also used for some recipes. The liqueur glasses used hold ¼ cup.

For sheet desserts you will need a 12 x 8 x 2-inch loose-bottom cake pan. For the triple chocolate mousses (see page 52) you will need a deep, 8-inch-square loose-bottom cake pan.

Mini desserts can be served in paper or foil petits fours or cupcake liners, or straight onto plates or mini cocktail paper napkins. Some can be served on forks or spoons.

Pastry bags and tips

Use a large nylon or waxed cotton pastry bag with a selection of plain or star tips. This is essential for piping mini éclairs (see page 76), meringues (see page 40), or for filling chocolate cups (see page 60) or filling glasses without creating smears.

For finer decorative work, wax paper or nonstick parchment paper pastry bags can be shaped into a cone from a double-thickness triangle of paper, filled, then the tip snipped away with scissors, saving the need for smaller piping tips. Plastic disposable pastry bags can be bought from specialty cookshops.

Cooking techniques

Freezing

If you are freezing desserts served in glasses, choose plastic glasses. Arrange the desserts on a baking sheet or in a plastic container and freeze them uncovered until firm, then cover with plastic wrap or the plastic container lid, seal, and label. Use within six weeks. Defrost desserts in the refrigerator overnight or at room temperature for 2 hours, then transfer to the refrigerator. If the desserts have been frozen, do not return any leftovers to the freezer.

Gelatin

This book uses powdered gelatin. Scoop the powder into a measuring teaspoon so it is level with the spoon, then sprinkle it over cold water in a small heatproof bowl. If specks remain on the surface of the water, gently stir them in using a teaspoon. Let the gelatin soak for 5 minutes (it forms a sponge-like mixture), then stand the bowl in a small saucepan and pour water into the pan halfway up the sides of the bowl. Gently simmer the water for 5 minutes, until the gelatin melts and you have a clear, straw-colored liquid. If it gets very hot, let it cool for a few minutes. Trickle the gelatin into your wine, juice, or cream, then pour the mixture straight into serving dishes (if the dessert contains sliced fruit, which may float, let it partly set before transferring it to the serving dishes). Chill in the refrigerator for 3–4 hours.

To invert the dessert, dip a metal mold into just-boiled water for 2 seconds (longer if it is silicone), then loosen the top of the dessert with your fingertips and invert the mold onto a serving plate. Holding the mold and plate, give a quick jerk, remove the mold, and clean the dish with paper towels. Serve within 30 minutes.

Caramel

The secret to caramel is to avoid stirring the sugar as it dissolves, because this can make it crystallize. Heat the sugar and water gently in a heavy saucepan, tilting it from time to time. Once the sugar has dissolved, boil rapidly for 4–5 minutes; the syrup will color around the edges and then will burn easily, so do not leave the pan unattended. Tilt the pan gently to encourage even coloring. When browned remove from the heat.

Meringues

Always use a clean, dry bowl and whisk. Whisk the egg whites until they form stiff, moist-looking peaks, then tilt the bowl; they won't move if they are ready. Gradually whisk in the sugar, a teaspoonful at a time, then continue to whisk for 1–2 minutes after it has been added to make the mixture smooth, thickened, and glossy. Spoon or pipe onto baking sheets lined with nonstick parchment paper and bake in a low oven, as specified in the recipe, until the meringues are crisp and can be lifted easily off the paper. If they are sticky on the bottom, cook for a few minutes longer, then try again. Cooled, unfilled meringues will keep in a cool place in a cookie jar layered with parchment paper for three to four days.

Lining pans

For square pans, place the pan on nonstick parchment paper, draw around it, and cut out the paper inside the lines. Cut a strip of paper the depth of the pan and make a ½-inch fold along one long edge. Grease the pan using a pastry brush, then fit the strip around the sides so the folded part sits on the bottom and snip the folded edge at the corners. Press the paper square into the bottom. For pans with round cups, grease the cups. Cut out circles of nonstick parchment paper ½ inch larger than the cup diameters. Make ¼-inch cuts at the sides of the circles and press them in so the snipped edges go up the sides.

Muffins and cupcakes

Muffins are made by adding the wet ingredients to the dry ones. The flour is usually sifted first. Add the wet ingredients all at once and fold everything together gently. As soon as they're combined but with specks of flour still visible, spoon the batter into the cups. Overmixing can make them heavy. Unless otherwise stated, fill cupcake liners until they're almost full and the mixture is level with the top of the liners. For muffins, the batter can extend above the tops of the cups slightly to achieve the "muffin top."

How to tell if a cake is cooked

When cooked, cakes are usually domed in the center with a lightly brown surface. Gently touch them with your fingers; they should feel just firm. Push a toothpick into the center; if cooked, it will come out clean.

Decoration techniques

Chocolate curls

Spread just-melted chocolate over a marble pastry board or cheese board in an even layer no less than ¼-inch thick. Let stand in a cool place to set. To make the curls, draw a long chef's knife across the chocolate at a 45-degree angle in a seesaw action to shave the chocolate into curls. For two-tone chocolate caraque, spread a band of melted white chocolate on the marble, let set for 5 minutes, then spread a band of melted dark chocolate onto it, butting up to the white chocolate, making sure that the level of the chocolate is the same for both types. Let stand to set, then shave into curls as above.

For speedy chocolate curls, turn a block of chocolate over so that the smooth underside is uppermost, then place the block on a cutting board and run a vegetable peeler firmly over the surface so that the blade is at a slight angle to the chocolate. The size of the curl that you make will depend on the temperature of the chocolate and the amount of fat it contains. If the chocolate is very cold, the curls will be tiny, so soften it in the microwave at full power for 10 seconds (if the bar is large or the chocolate is dark, you may need to give it a second burst in the microwave). The fewer cocoa solids the chocolate contains, the easier it will be to shape, so white and milk chocolate will make larger curls than dark chocolate.

Piped chocolate

Spoon melted chocolate into a small nonstick parchment paper pastry bag (see page 6), roll down the top to enclose the chocolate, then snip a little off the tip of the bag. There is no need to add a piping tip. Pipe shapes, such as leaves, flowers, butterflies, initials, and hearts, over nonstick parchment paper freehand, or draw them on a second sheet of paper, using a black pen, then slide it under the top sheet before piping. Fill in the shapes with extra piped squiggles of chocolate or flood the center to fill it completely.

Colored chocolate

Melted white chocolate can be colored with the tiniest amount of liquid food coloring and can make an eye-catching decoration piped over a layer of dark chocolate.

Sugar decorations

Ready-to-use fondant can be left white or colored with paste or gel food colorings before being shaped. Don't use liquid food colorings, because these will make the fondant sticky and difficult to roll out. Paste or gel colors can be bought from some large supermarkets, specialty cook shops, or online in a wide variety of colors. Apply the coloring to the fondant on the end of a toothpick and use sparingly. Knead the coloring in, then roll out the fondant thinly and stamp out stars, holly leaves, snowflakes, or tiny hearts or flowers, using cutters. (Look out for mini plunger flower cutters, because these can be depressed into a small circle of foam for a curved flower effect). Let the decorations dry at room temperature on a baking sheet lined with nonstick parchment paper, then store them in a small plastic container, interleaved with extra paper, for up to two months. You can also buy prepared sugar flowers or choose from a range of edible glitter, sugar strands, or tiny shapes from supermarkets or specialty suppliers.

natural flower decorations

Tiny flowers can add a delicate finishing touch to a miniature dessert, but first make sure that they are edible. Choose from tiny viola or pansy flowers in a mix of colors to borage, violet, little rose petals, herb flowers or tiny mint leaves. Brush petals or leaves lightly with a little beaten egg white, then sprinkle with superfine sugar and let dry on a baking sheet lined with nonstick parchment paper for an hour. Use immediately.

Citrus curls

Pare away the rind from lemons, oranges, or limes with a zester (a small metal-topped tool with a row of holes punched in the top). Dust the curls with a little superfine sugar and sprinkle them over mousses or ice creams. For larger, corkscrew-type curls, remove the citrus peel in single, slightly larger strips with a canelle knife, then twist each strip tightly around a toothpick, let stand for a minute, slide the toothpick out, and hang the corkscrew curl over the edge of the serving dish.

Caramel shards

Just-cooked caramel can be drizzled over nonstick parchment paper, then left to cool and harden. When ready to serve, break it into shards or chop it into small pieces. For extra interest, you can also add chopped or slivered nuts to the caramel before it hardens.

Mini Comfort Treats

Blueberry and maple syrup pancakes

Makes: 30
Prep: 20 minutes
Cook: 10–15 minutes

Popular with diners of all ages, these bite-size pancakes take only a few minutes to prepare — which is just as well, because chances are they will disappear as soon as they are cooked.

1½ cups all-purpose flour

1 teaspoon baking powder

½ teaspoon baking soda

1 tablespoon granulated sugar

2 eggs, separated

finely grated rind of 1 lemon and juice of ½ lemon

1 cup milk

¾ cup blueberries

a little sunflower oil, for frying

maple syrup, to serve

crème fraîche or whipped cream, to serve (optional)

1. Put the flour, baking powder, and baking soda into a mixing bowl, then stir in the sugar. Whisk the egg whites in a separate large, clean mixing bowl until you have soft peaks.

2. Add the egg yolks, lemon rind, and lemon juice to the flour, then gradually whisk in the milk until smooth. Fold in a spoonful of the whisked egg whites, then add the rest and fold in gently. Sprinkle the blueberries into the bowl, then gently and briefly fold them in.

3. Pour a little oil into a large skillet, then place it over medium heat. When it's hot, drop tablespoonfuls of the blueberry batter into the skillet, leaving a little space between the pancakes. Cook for 2–3 minutes, until bubbles appear on the surface of the pancakes and the undersides are golden. Turn the pancakes over and cook the second side for 1–2 minutes, until golden.

4. Remove the pancakes from the skillet, using a spatula, and keep them hot in a clean dish towel. Cook the remaining blueberry batter in batches of 10 pancakes at a time, until all the mixture is cooked, oiling the skillet as needed.

5. Transfer the pancakes to small dessert plates, serving 4–5 pancakes per serving. Drizzle a little maple syrup over them and serve extra syrup in a small pitcher. Top the pancakes with teaspoonfuls of crème fraîche, if desired.

Cherry and almond cakes

Makes: 18
Prep: 25 minutes
Cook: 12–15 minutes

Make these cakes when cherries are in season, or cheat and use canned cherries that have been well drained. Serve them still warm from the oven, with a little dish of crème fraîche on the side, if desired.

4 tablespoons unsalted butter, softened, plus extra for greasing

¼ cup granulated sugar

½ cup all-purpose flour

¼ cup almond meal (ground almonds)

¾ teaspoon baking powder

1 egg

a few drops of almond extract

18 fresh cherries, stemmed and pitted, or 18 canned cherries

¼ cup slivered almonds

confectioners' sugar, sifted, for dusting

crème fraîche or whipped cream, to serve (optional)

1. Preheat the oven to 350°F. Lightly grease 18 cups of two 12-cup mini muffin pans with butter.

2. Put the butter, sugar, flour, almond meal, and baking powder into a mixing bowl, then stir. Add the egg and almond extract and beat together briefly using a wooden spoon, until smooth.

3. Spoon the mixture into the muffin pan cups, then lightly press a cherry into the center of each cake. Sprinkle with the slivered almonds. Bake in the preheated oven for 12–15 minutes, or until risen and firm to the touch.

4. Let the cakes stand in the pan for 5 minutes, then loosen with a blunt knife and transfer to a wire rack to cool. Serve warm, dusted with sifted confectioners' sugar, with spoonfuls of crème fraîche, if desired.

Berry and oat crisps

Makes: 8
Prep: 20 minutes
Cook: 20 minutes

These comforting little desserts are always a great hit. If you prefer, make double the amount of the crumble topping and store it in the freezer, then use it at a later date and bake from frozen.

7 red plums (about 1 pound), halved, pitted, and diced

1 cup raspberries

2 tablespoons packed light brown sugar

3 tablespoons water

custard or heavy cream, to serve

TOPPING

¾ cup all-purpose flour

¼ cup rolled oats

½ cup barley flakes

3 tablespoons packed light brown sugar

3 tablespoons unsalted butter, chilled and diced

1. Preheat the oven to 350°F. Put the plums, raspberries, sugar, and water into a heavy saucepan. Cover and simmer for 5 minutes, or until the fruit has softened.

2. For the topping, put the flour, rolled oats, barley flakes, and sugar into a mixing bowl and stir. Rub in the butter, using your fingertips, until the mixture resembles fine crumbs.

3. Spoon the fruit mixture into eight ⅔-cup metal molds and stand them on a baking sheet. Sprinkle the topping on top.

4. Bake in the preheated oven for 15 minutes, or until golden. Let the crisps cool for 5–10 minutes, then serve topped with small spoonfuls of custard or cream.

Cinnamon and apple fritters with blackberry sauce

Makes: 30
Prep: 30 minutes
Cook: 20–35 minutes

A retro dessert that uses staple ingredients. It's a good way to make the most of blackberries you have in the freezer. Alternatively, use whatever frozen berries you have on hand — raspberries or blueberries would work well.

8 small apples, such as Pippin

1 cup blackberries

½ cup water

⅓ cup granulated sugar

1¼ cups all-purpose flour

a large pinch of ground cinnamon

1 egg, separated

⅔ cup milk

4 cups sunflower oil

1. For the sauce, quarter, core, peel, and dice 2 of the apples, then put them into a heavy saucepan. Add the blackberries, water, and a tablespoon of the sugar. Cover and simmer for 5–10 minutes, or until the apples have softened. Puree until smooth using an immersion blender, then press through a strainer into a serving bowl to remove the seeds. Cover with plastic wrap and set aside.

2. Peel and core the remaining apples, cut them into thin rings, then put them in a plastic bag with ⅓ cup of the flour. Seal the bag, then shake to thinly coat the apples with the flour.

3. Put the remaining flour into a mixing bowl. Stir in a tablespoon of the sugar, the cinnamon, and the egg yolk. Gradually whisk in the milk until smooth.

4. Whisk the egg white in a separate large, clean mixing bowl until you have soft peaks. Fold it into the flour mixture.

5. Pour the oil into a saucepan, making sure that it is filled no more than halfway. Heat to 325°F on a candy thermometer, or until bubbles form when a little batter is dropped into the oil. Line a plate with paper towels.

6. Shake any excess flour from the apple slices, then dip them into the batter and remove them using 2 forks. Drain off the excess batter, then carefully add 4–5 apple slices to the hot oil and cook for 2–3 minutes, or until golden. Lift out of the oil with a draining spoon, then transfer to the lined plate and let drain while you cook the remaining apples in batches of this size.

7. Sprinkle the remaining sugar over the fritters and serve with the blackberry sauce for dipping.

S'mores

Makes: 18
Prep: 25 minutes
Cook: 12–15 minutes

Inspired by s'mores traditionally cooked over a campfire, this recipe uses homemade buttery cookies for sandwiching marshmallows, which are topped with melting chocolate.

a little sunflower oil, for greasing

1½ cups whole-wheat flour, plus extra for dusting

2 teaspoons baking powder

½ cup rolled oats

¼ cup granulated sugar

1¼ sticks unsalted butter, chilled and diced

2 egg yolks

8 ounces semisweet dark chocolate, broken into 18 pieces

18 marshmallows

1. Preheat the oven to 350°F. Lightly brush 2 baking sheets with oil.

2. Put the flour, baking powder, oats, and sugar into a mixing bowl, then stir. Rub in the butter, using your fingertips, until the mixture resembles fine crumbs. Stir in the egg yolks and press together, using your hands, to make a ball of dough.

3. Lightly dust a work surface with flour. Knead the dough lightly, then roll it out thinly. Stamp out 2¼-inch circles, using a cookie cutter, and transfer to the prepared baking sheets. Shape the remaining dough into a ball, knead it, then roll it out thinly again and stamp out more cookies. Continue until all the dough has been used.

4. Bake in the preheated oven for 12–15 minutes, or until golden brown, then let cool a little.

5. Add a piece of chocolate to half the hot cookies and a marshmallow to the other half. Let stand for 1–2 minutes, or until the chocolate just begins to melt, then sandwich together the cookies in pairs so that the marshmallows are in the center and the chocolate on top. Serve warm or cold.

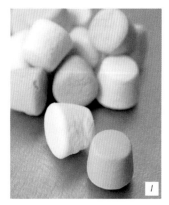

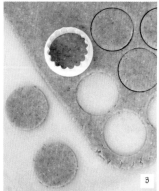

Hot orange soufflés with chocolate and orange sauce

Makes: 12
Prep: 25 minutes
Cook: 20–25 minutes

Serving hot soufflés adds a touch of suspense to any meal because they puff up dramatically in the oven but can fall just as quickly. Get your dinner guests ready and waiting, dust the tops of the soufflés with a speedy flourish of confectioners' sugar, then serve, hopefully to applause.

2 tablespoons unsalted butter, for greasing

½ cup superfine sugar, plus 2 tablespoons for sprinkling

3 eggs, separated, plus 1 extra egg white

⅓ cup all-purpose flour

1 cup milk

finely grated rind of 1 large orange

⅓ cup orange juice, or 3 tablespoons orange juice plus 2 tablespoons Cointreau

a large pinch of ground cinnamon

confectioners' sugar, sifted, for dusting

SAUCE

6 ounces semisweet dark chocolate, coarsely chopped

¼ cup orange juice

2 tablespoons superfine sugar

1. Grease 12 wide-topped, ½-cup ovenproof demitasse coffee cups with the butter, then sprinkle them with 2 tablespoons of superfine sugar, tilting to coat them evenly. Put them on a baking sheet and set aside.

2. Put half the measured sugar and all the egg yolks into a mixing bowl and beat together for 2 minutes, using an electric handheld mixer, until thick and pale. Sift the flour over the surface, then fold it in.

3. Pour the milk into a medium, heavy saucepan, bring just to a boil, then gradually whisk it into the egg mixture until smooth. Pour the mixture back into the pan, then cook over low heat, whisking gently, until thickened and smooth.

4. Remove the soufflé mixture from the heat and whisk in the orange rind, juice, Cointreau if using, and cinnamon. Cover with plastic wrap and let cool.

5. Preheat the oven to 375°F. Whisk the egg whites in a large, clean mixing bowl until you have stiff, moist-looking peaks. Gradually whisk in the remaining sugar, a teaspoonful at a time. Fold the whites into the cooled soufflé mixture, then divide among the 12 dishes so that they are three-quarters full. Bake in the preheated oven for 15–20 minutes, or until the soufflés are well risen, the tops are golden, and they are almost set in the center.

6. Meanwhile, to make the sauce, put the chocolate, orange juice, and sugar in a heatproof bowl, set the bowl over a saucepan of gently simmering water, and heat until smooth and melted, stirring from time to time. Pour into a pitcher.

7. Quickly serve the soufflés on saucers, dusted with sifted confectioners' sugar, and drizzle the warm chocolate sauce over the top.

Cranberry and granola sundaes

Makes: 10
Prep: 20 minutes
Cook: 13-15 minutes

With the mix of tangy, slightly sharp cranberry compote, creamy smooth Greek yogurt, and crunchy granola, this is a great dessert or party brunch. Make up extra granola and serve in little dishes as an alternative to chips.

a little sunflower oil, for greasing

2 tablespoons sesame seeds

2 tablespoons pumpkin seeds

¼ cup rolled oats

¼ cup slivered almonds

3 tablespoons unsalted butter

2 tablespoons honey

2 tablespoons packed light brown sugar

1 cup honey-flavored Greek yogurt

CRANBERRY COMPOTE

2 teaspoons cornstarch

⅓ cup firmly packed light brown sugar

juice of 1 large orange

2 cups frozen cranberries

1. Preheat the oven to 350°F. Lightly brush a large baking sheet with oil.

2. Put the sesame seeds, pumpkin seeds, rolled oats, and slivered almonds into a bowl and mix together using your fingertips. Put the butter, honey, and sugar into a heavy saucepan and heat gently until the butter has melted and the sugar dissolved. Remove from the heat and stir in the seed mixture. Tip onto the prepared baking sheet and spread into a thin, even layer. Bake in the preheated oven for 8-10 minutes, stirring halfway through cooking and moving the browned edges to the center. Let cool in the pan.

3. For the cranberry compote, put the cornstarch, sugar, and orange juice into a heavy saucepan and cook over medium heat, stirring, until smooth. Add the frozen cranberries and cook, uncovered, for 5 minutes, stirring, until they have softened and the juices have thickened. Let cool.

4. Crumble half the granola, using your fingertips, and break the rest into shards. Sprinkle a layer of the crumble into 10 shot glasses, spoon a layer of yogurt over the granola, then add a layer of cranberry compote. Repeat the layers, finishing with a layer of compote, and decorate with the shards of granola. Any remaining granola shards can be served in a small separate dish.

Chocolate molten lava cakes with caramel sauce

Makes: 10
Prep: 25 minutes
Chill: 1 hour or overnight
Cook: 17-20 minutes

This restaurant favorite is surprisingly easy to make, and it can be prepared in advance and stored in the refrigerator for up to 24 hours. The secret is to bake the desserts for the precise amount of cooking time and to test one before serving them. They should be crusty on top but soft and molten in the center.

1¼ sticks unsalted butter

4 teaspoons unsweetened cocoa powder

6 ounces semisweet dark chocolate, coarsely chopped

2 eggs, plus 2 egg yolks

⅔ cup superfine sugar

3 tablespoons all-purpose flour

confectioners' sugar, sifted, for dusting

CARAMEL SAUCE

4 tablespoons unsalted butter

¼ cup firmly packed light brown sugar

1 tablespoon honey

⅔ cup heavy cream

1. Melt 2 tablespoons of the butter in a small saucepan, then brush it over the insides of ten ½-cup ovenproof ramekins (individual ceramic dishes). Sift a little cocoa into each ramekin, then tilt to coat the bottom and sides evenly, tapping out any excess.

2. Put the chocolate and remaining stick of butter in a heatproof bowl, set the bowl over a saucepan of gently simmering water, and heat until melted, stirring from time to time.

3. Put the eggs, egg yolks, and superfine sugar into a mixing bowl and whisk together until thick and frothy and the whisk leaves a trail when raised above the mixture. Sift over the flour, then gently fold it in.

4. Fold the melted chocolate mixture into the egg mixture until smooth. Pour it into the prepared ramekins, cover, and chill in the refrigerator for 1 hour, or overnight if time permits.

5. For the caramel sauce, put the butter, light brown sugar, and honey into a heavy saucepan and heat gently for 3-4 minutes, or until the butter has melted and the sugar dissolved, then boil for 1-2 minutes, stirring, until it begins to smell of caramel and thicken. Remove from the heat and stir in the cream.

6. Preheat the oven to 350°F. Take the ramekins out of the refrigerator and let them stand at room temperature for 10 minutes. Bake in the preheated oven for 10-12 minutes, or until well risen, the tops are crusty, and the centers still slightly soft. Reheat the sauce over low heat, if needed.

7. Dust the desserts with sifted confectioners' sugar. Serve with the sauce in a pitcher for guests to pour on.

Mini Indulgent Treats

Raspberry and strawberry meringues

Makes: 20
Prep: 25 minutes
Cook: 25–30 minutes

Spoil the ones you love with these gorgeous meringues. You can make them in advance and keep them in an airtight container for several days, then just make the topping when you are ready to serve them.

2 egg whites

½ cup superfine sugar

½ teaspoon cornstarch

½ teaspoon white wine vinegar

TOPPING

1¼ cups heavy cream

finely grated rind and juice of
1 lime

3 tablespoons strawberry jam or
strawberry preserves

1½ cups raspberries

1½ cups hulled and sliced,
small strawberries

1. Preheat the oven to 275°F. Line a large baking sheet with nonstick parchment paper.

2. Whisk the egg whites in a large, clean mixing bowl until you have stiff, moist-looking peaks. Gradually whisk in the sugar a tablespoonful at a time. Once all the sugar has been added, whisk for an additional 1–2 minutes, until the meringue is thick and glossy.

3. Mix together the cornstarch and vinegar in a small bowl until smooth, then fold it into the meringue. Spoon the mixture onto the prepared baking sheet in 20 mounds, leaving a little space between each mound. Spread it into circles 2 inches in diameter, then make a small dip in the center of each circle using the back of a teaspoon.

4. Bake in the preheated oven for 25–30 minutes, or until the meringues are a pale cookie color and can easily be lifted off the paper. If they stick to the paper, cook them for another few minutes, then retest. Let cool on the paper.

5. For the topping, pour the cream into a large mixing bowl and whisk until it forms soft swirls, then fold in the lime rind. Spoon a dollop of the cream onto the top of each meringue, then transfer to a serving plate.

6. Put the jam and lime juice in a small, heavy saucepan and place over gentle heat until the jam has just melted. Stir in the raspberries and strawberries, then let cool a little. Spoon the fruit over the meringues and serve.

Strawberry and rosé gelatins

Makes: 8
Prep: 20 minutes
Cook: 5 minutes
Chill: 4 hours

A pretty finale to any summer celebration. If you have roses in the yard, you may want to decorate the cream with tiny, pink rose petals instead of finely grated lemon rind.

1 cup hulled and sliced,
small strawberries

1½ tablespoons superfine sugar

3 tablespoons water

2 teaspoons powdered gelatin

1 cup rosé wine

TOPPING

1½ tablespoons superfine sugar

2 tablespoons rosé wine

finely grated rind of 1 lemon

⅔ cup heavy cream

1. Put the strawberries and sugar into a mixing bowl and mix together using a metal spoon.

2. Put the water in a small heatproof bowl, then sprinkle the gelatin over the surface, making sure the powder is absorbed. Set aside for 5 minutes. Set the bowl of gelatin in a saucepan of gently simmering water and heat for about 5 minutes, stirring from time to time, until the gelatin is a clear liquid (see page 7).

3. Divide the sugar-coated strawberries between 8 small champagne or liqueur glasses. Pour the wine into a small bowl or liquid measuring cup and stir in the gelatin, then pour it into the glasses. Cover and chill in the refrigerator for 4 hours, or until the gelatin has set.

4. To make the topping, put the sugar, wine, and half the lemon rind into a small bowl and stir. Pour the cream into a large mixing bowl and whisk until it forms soft swirls. Add the wine mixture and whisk briefly, until the cream is thick again. Spoon the lemon cream into the center of the desserts, then decorate with the remaining lemon rind.

Rippled raspberry cheesecakes

Makes: 12
Prep: 30 minutes
Cook: 5 minutes
Chill: 3 hours

Silicone sheets make inverting these dainty desserts out of the cups child's play. The swirled effect is simple to create but looks really impressive.

4 cups unsalted butter

1 cup crushed graham crackers

3 tablespoons water

2 teaspoons powdered gelatin

1 cup raspberries, plus 24 to decorate

⅔ cup heavy cream

⅔ cup prepared custard or vanilla pudding

¼ teaspoon vanilla extract

1. Melt the butter in a saucepan, then stir in the graham cracker crumbs. Divide the mixture among the sections of two 6-cup silicone muffin pans; the bottom of each cup should be 1½ inches in diameter. Press over the bottom of the cups using the back of a teaspoon, then chill in the refrigerator.

2. Put the water in a small heatproof bowl, then sprinkle the gelatin over the surface, making sure the powder is absorbed. Set aside for 5 minutes. Meanwhile, puree the 1 cup of raspberries in a blender, then press through a strainer into a bowl to remove the seeds. Set the bowl of gelatin in a saucepan of gently simmering water and heat for about 5 minutes, stirring from time to time, until the gelatin is a clear liquid (see page 7).

3. Pour the cream into a large mixing bowl and whisk until it forms soft swirls. Fold in the custard or vanilla pudding and vanilla extract. Stir 1½ tablespoons of the gelatin into the raspberry puree and fold the rest into the cream mixture. Spoon the cream mixture into the muffin cups, level the surface using the back of a teaspoon, then spoon the raspberry puree on top. Swirl together the 2 mixtures using the handle of the teaspoon. Cover and chill in the refrigerator for 3 hours, or longer if time permits, until set.

4. To serve, loosen the desserts using a blunt knife, then invert them out by pressing underneath. Decorate each dessert with 2 raspberries.

Lemon and blueberry duets

Makes: 10
Prep: 15 minutes
Cook: 5 minutes
Chill: 1–2 hours

1¼ cups heavy cream

½ cup superfine or
granulated sugar

finely grated rind and juice of
1 lemon, plus grated rind of
1 lemon to decorate

1 teaspoon cornstarch

¼ cup water

2¾ cups blueberries

*If you need a dessert in a hurry, then this is it.
It takes just 20 minutes to make, then can be
kept in the refrigerator to chill until you are
ready to serve.*

1. Put the cream and ⅓ cup sugar into a medium, heavy saucepan, then heat gently, stirring, until the sugar has dissolved. Increase the heat and bring to a boil, then cook for 1 minute, stirring.

2. Remove from the heat, add half the finely grated lemon rind and all the juice, and stir continuously for 1 minute, until the mixture begins to thicken slightly. Pour into 10 shot glasses, then let cool.

3. Put the remaining sugar and finely grated lemon rind into a smaller heavy saucepan, stir in the cornstarch, then gradually mix in the water until smooth. Add half the blueberries, then place over medium heat and cook, stirring, for 3–4 minutes, until they are starting to soften and the sauce thicken.

4. Remove the compote from the heat, stir in the remaining blueberries, then let cool. Cover the glasses and blueberry compote with plastic wrap, then transfer to the refrigerator for 1–2 hours, or until set.

5. When ready to serve, stir the blueberries, then spoon them into the glasses and decorate with the grated lemon rind.

White chocolate and strawberry cheesecakes

Makes: 40
Prep: 30 minutes
Cook: 45–50 minutes
Chill: overnight

An all-American favorite, this baked cheesecake tastes even better the day after it is made.

SPONGE CAKE

4 tablespoons margarine, softened

¼ cup superfine or granulated sugar

½ cup all-purpose flour

¾ teaspoon baking powder

1 egg

CHEESECAKE

8 ounces white chocolate, coarsely chopped

2½ cups cream cheese

⅓ cup superfine or granulated sugar

1 teaspoon vanilla extract

1 cup heavy cream

4 eggs

TOPPING

1 cup crème fraîche or whipped cream

10 strawberries, hulled and quartered

2 ounces white chocolate, cut into shards using a swivel vegetable peeler

1. Preheat the oven to 350°F. Line a 12 x 8 x 2-inch loose-bottom cake pan with nonstick parchment paper, snipping diagonally into the corners, then pressing the paper into the pan so that the bottom and sides are lined.

2. Put all the sponge ingredients into a mixing bowl and beat together using a wooden spoon until smooth. Spoon the batter into the prepared pan and spread it into a thin layer using a spatula. Bake in the preheated oven for 10–12 minutes, or until golden and firm to the touch. Remove from the oven and let cool. Reduce the oven temperature to 300°F.

3. For the cheesecake, put the chocolate in a heatproof bowl, set the bowl over a saucepan of gently simmering water, and heat until melted. Stir briefly and let cool. Meanwhile, put the cream cheese, sugar, and vanilla extract into a mixing bowl and beat together briefly, using an electric handheld mixer, until just smooth. Gradually beat in the cream until thick once again. Beat in the eggs, one at a time, waiting until the mixture is smooth before adding the next one. Stir in the melted chocolate.

4. Spoon the cheesecake mixture onto the sponge and spread it out so it forms an even layer. Bake in the preheated oven for 30–35 minutes, or until the edge is slightly cracked and the center still a little soft. Turn off the oven, leave the door ajar, and let it cool in the oven.

5. Cover the cheesecake and put it in the refrigerator overnight. When ready to serve, remove the cheesecake from the pan, peel off the parchment paper, and cut into 40 squares. Put these on a serving plate and top each square with a spoonful of crème fraîche. Add a quarter of a strawberry to each square and sprinkle with white chocolate shards.

Apricot and chocolate meringues

Makes: 12
Prep: 20 minutes
Cook: 10–13 minutes

Quick and easy to make, these pretty desserts look wonderful served on a plate or platter. When apricots are out of season, try making these with halved plums.

6 apricots, halved and pitted

juice of ½ small orange

1 egg white

2 tablespoons superfine sugar

2 ounces semisweet dark chocolate, cut into 12 pieces

1. Preheat the oven to 350°F.

2. Arrange the apricots, cut side up, on a baking sheet. Drizzle the orange juice over the top of them. Bake in the preheated oven for 5–8 minutes.

3. Meanwhile, whisk the egg white in a large, clean mixing bowl until you have stiff, moist-looking peaks. Gradually whisk in the sugar a teaspoonful at a time. Once all the sugar has been added, whisk for an additional 1–2 minutes, until the meringue is thick and glossy.

4. Spoon the meringue into a pastry bag fitted with a medium star tip. Put a piece of chocolate in the center of each apricot.

5. If the apricots wobble, stick them to the baking sheet with a little meringue. Pipe a whirl of meringue on top of the chocolate. Bake in the preheated oven for 5 minutes, or until the meringue is tinged golden brown and just cooked. Let cool for a few minutes, then transfer to a serving plate.

Baby blueberry brûlées

Makes: 12
Prep: 20 minutes
Cook: 15 minutes
Chill: 3-4 hours

This is a girlie dessert, in health-conscious-size servings — although it will be hard to resist the temptation of second helpings!

1 cup blueberries

4 egg yolks

1 teaspoon vanilla extract

½ cup superfine or granulated sugar

1¼ cups heavy cream

1. Preheat the oven to 325°F. Put twelve ¼-cup ovenproof dishes in a large roasting pan and divide the blueberries among them.

2. Put the egg yolks, vanilla, and 3 tablespoons of sugar into a small bowl and mix together, using a fork, until smooth and creamy. Pour the cream into a small, heavy saucepan, bring to a boil, then gradually mix it into the yolks. Strain the mixture through a strainer back into the pan before pouring it back into the bowl.

3. Pour the cream mixture over the blueberries. Pour warm water into the roasting pan to come halfway up the sides of the dishes. Bake in the preheated oven for 15 minutes, or until the custard is just set, with a slight wobble in the center.

4. Let cool for 5–10 minutes, then lift the dishes out of the water and transfer to the refrigerator to chill for 3-4 hours.

5. To serve, sprinkle the remaining sugar over the dishes in an even layer, then caramelize it using a cook's blow torch or under a broiler preheated to hot.

Chocolate and ginger refrigerator cake

Makes: 36
Prep: 25 minutes
Cook: 6-7 minutes
Chill: 3-4 hours

For those moments when you really need a chocolate fix, this no-bake dessert fits the bill. Rich, dark, and supremely chocolatey, it has a hint of ginger that contrasts well with the crunch of crushed cookies.

½ cup hazelnuts

8 ounces semisweet dark chocolate, coarsely chopped

1 stick unsalted butter

1 (14-ounce) can sweetened condensed milk

2 cups crushed graham crackers

1 cup diced dried apricots

4 pieces preserved ginger from a jar, drained and finely chopped

2 ounces milk chocolate, coarsely chopped

1. Line a shallow, 8-inch-square cake pan with nonstick parchment paper, snipping diagonally into the corners, then pressing the paper into the pan so that the bottom and sides are lined. Preheat the broiler to medium. Put the hazelnuts on a baking sheet and toast under the broiler for 3–4 minutes, or until golden, shaking them halfway through.

2. Put the dark chocolate, butter, and condensed milk into a heavy saucepan and heat gently, stirring all the time, until the chocolate and butter have melted. Spoon one-fifth of the mixture into a bowl, cover, and set aside.

3. Put the toasted hazelnuts, graham cracker crumbs, dried apricots, and preserved ginger into the remaining chocolate mixture, then stir well. Transfer the mixture to the prepared cake pan and press it into an even layer.

4. Spoon the reserved chocolate mixture over the top of the refrigerator cake in a thin, even layer, then chill in the refrigerator for 3 hours, or until set.

5. Put the milk chocolate in a heatproof bowl, set the bowl over a saucepan of gently simmering water, and heat until melted, then stir. Put the melted chocolate into a paper pastry bag and snip off the tip, then pipe swirls onto the refrigerator cake (see page 8). Chill in the refrigerator for 15 minutes, then lift the cake out of the pan, peel off the paper, and cut into 36 squares.

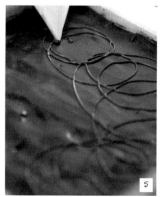

5

Mini Special Occasion Treats

Berry torte

Makes: 20
Prep: 40 minutes
Cook: 25–30 minutes

Spoil the ones you love with these dainty, rich, dark chocolate cakes layered with minty strawberries and swirled with rich chocolate cream. If you don't have a heart-shape cookie cutter, use a small round one instead.

1 cup unsweetened cocoa powder

1 cup boiling water

1 stick unsalted butter, softened

1 cup firmly packed light brown sugar

2 eggs, beaten

1 2/3 cups all-purpose flour

1 teaspoon baking powder

FILLING

2/3 cup heavy cream

3/4 cup hulled and finely chopped strawberries

1 tablespoon finely chopped fresh mint

1 tablespoon superfine or granulated sugar

FROSTING

2/3 cup heavy cream

6 ounces semisweet dark chocolate, coarsely chopped

1. Preheat the oven to 350°F. Line a deep, 10-inch-square, loose-bottom cake pan with nonstick parchment paper, snipping diagonally into the corners, then pressing the paper into the pan so that the bottom and sides are lined.

2. Put the cocoa in a heatproof bowl, then gradually stir in the boiling water until you have a smooth paste. Let cool.

3. Put the butter and light brown sugar into a mixing bowl and beat together using an electric handheld mixer until light and fluffy. Gradually beat in the eggs and a tablespoon of flour, until smooth. Sift the remaining flour and the baking powder into the bowl and fold them in, then gradually stir in the cooled cocoa mixture.

4. Pour the batter into the prepared cake pan and spread into an even layer using a spatula. Bake in the preheated oven for 25–30 minutes, or until risen and firm to the touch and a toothpick inserted into the center of the cake comes out clean. Let cool for 10 minutes, then transfer to a wire rack and let cool completely.

5. Remove the parchment paper and, using a 2-inch heart-shape cutter, cut out 20 cakes. Cut each cake in half horizontally.

6. For the filling, pour the cream into a large mixing bowl and whisk until it forms soft swirls. Fold in the strawberries, mint, and superfine sugar, then spread the mixture over the bottom half of each cake and top with the other cake half. Put the cakes on a wire rack.

7. For the frosting, pour the cream into a small, heavy saucepan and bring just to a boil. Remove from the heat and add the chocolate. Set aside for 5 minutes, then stir until smooth and glossy. Let cool for an additional 15 minutes, until thick, then spoon onto, and spread over, the top of the cakes. Let set, then transfer to a serving plate.

Strawberry and mint ice cream cones

Makes: 24
Prep: 40 minutes
Cook: 15–20 minutes
Freeze: 6 hours 20 minutes

These pretty cones would be fun to serve at a family summer party. Keep a few of them in the freezer for a special last-minute treat to thrill any little girl and her friends.

CONES

4 tablespoons unsalted butter

2 egg whites

½ cup superfine or granulated sugar

a few drops of vanilla extract

½ cup all-purpose flour

ICE CREAM

½ cup superfine or granulated sugar

⅓ cup water

2 sprigs of mint

3 cups hulled and sliced strawberries (about 1 pound), plus extra to serve

1 tablespoon powdered gelatin

⅔ cup heavy cream

1. Preheat the oven to 350°F. Line 3 baking sheets with nonstick parchment paper. You will need 8 homemade cones made out of cardboard covered with parchment paper to use as molds.

2. For the cones, melt the butter in a saucepan. Lightly whisk the egg whites in a large, clean mixing bowl until frothy but still translucent. Whisk in the sugar, then the melted butter and the vanilla. Sift in the flour, then fold it in until smooth. Drop 4–5 half-teaspoonfuls of the batter over one of the prepared baking sheets and spread each into a circle 2–2½ inches in diameter. Bake in the preheated oven for 3–5 minutes, or until just golden at the edges.

3. Let the baked cookies harden for a few moments, then loosen with a spatula and quickly shape into small cones around the molds. Let set for 1–2 minutes, then remove the molds. Repeat baking and shaping cones until all the batter is used, then let cool. Don't bake too many cookies at once, or they will harden before you can shape them.

4. For the ice cream, put the sugar, 2 tablespoons of water, and the mint into a medium, heavy saucepan. Heat gently, stirring from time to time, until the sugar has dissolved. Add the sliced strawberries, increase the heat slightly, and cook for 3 minutes. Discard the mint, then puree the mixture in a blender until smooth. Press the puree through a strainer into a metal loaf pan.

5. Put the remaining water in a small heatproof bowl, then sprinkle the gelatin over the surface, making sure the powder is absorbed. Set aside for 5 minutes. Set the bowl of gelatin in a saucepan of gently simmering water and heat for about 5 minutes, stirring from time to time, until the gelatin is a clear liquid (see page 7). Gently stir the gelatin into the pureed strawberry mixture, let cool, then freeze for 20 minutes.

6. Pour the cream in a large mixing bowl and whisk until it forms soft swirls. Transfer the just-setting strawberry mixture to another large mixing bowl and whisk for a few minutes. Fold the cream into the strawberries. Stand the cones in small cups and pipe the ice cream into them. Freeze for 6 hours or overnight. To serve, arrange the cones in a glass bowl with extra strawberries.

Triple chocolate mousses

Makes: 36
Prep: 45 minutes
Cook: 2 minutes
Chill: overnight
Freeze: 45 minutes

These fancy-looking desserts can be prepared the day before you plan to serve them, or even frozen, and are easier to slice if not fully defrosted.

4 tablespoons unsalted butter

1 tablespoon unsweetened cocoa powder

1¼ cups crushed graham crackers

milk chocolate curls, to decorate

MOUSSE

¼ cup water

4 teaspoons powdered gelatin

4 ounces semisweet dark chocolate, coarsely chopped

4 ounces milk chocolate, coarsely chopped

4 ounces white chocolate, coarsely chopped

1 stick unsalted butter

⅓ cup milk

6 eggs, separated

½ teaspoon vanilla extract

1½ cups heavy cream

1. Line a deep, 8-inch-square, loose-bottom cake pan with 2 long strips of plastic wrap, laid over each other in a cross, then press into the pan. The edges of the plastic wrap should hang over the sides of the pan.

2. Melt the butter in a small saucepan, then stir in the cocoa and graham cracker crumbs. Press the mixture into the pan in an even layer, then cover and chill in the refrigerator.

3. For the mousse, put the water in a small heatproof bowl, then sprinkle the gelatin over the surface, making sure the powder is absorbed. Set aside for 5 minutes. Set the bowl of gelatin in a saucepan of gently simmering water and heat for 5 mintes, stirring from time to time, until the gelatin is a clear liquid (see page 7).

4. Put each type of chopped chocolate in a different heatproof bowl, then add one-third of the butter and 2 tablespoons of milk to each bowl. Place each bowl over a saucepan of gently simmering water and heat until the chocolate has melted. Stir 2 egg yolks into each bowl, 1 at a time, then remove from the heat.

5. Stir 4 teaspoons of the dissolved gelatin into each bowl, then stir the vanilla into the white chocolate. Pour the cream into a fourth bowl and whisk until it forms soft swirls. Fold one-third of the cream into each of the chocolate mixtures. Whisk the egg whites in a large, clean mixing bowl until you have soft peaks, then divide them among the chocolate bowls and fold in gently.

6. Pour the dark chocolate mousse into the graham cracker-lined pan, spread it into an even layer, then freeze for 15 minutes. Spoon over the white chocolate layer and freeze for 30 minutes. Gently whisk the milk chocolate layer to soften, if needed, then spoon it over and chill in the refrigerator overnight, or until set.

7. To serve, lift the mousse out of the pan, pressing from the bottom. Peel off the plastic wrap. Cut the mousse into 6 strips, using a wet knife, then cut each strip into 6 small squares, wiping and wetting the knife frequently so that the layers don't become smeared. Arrange on small plates or saucers and decorate with milk chocolate curls.

Shortbread stacks

Makes: 24
Prep: 40 minutes
Cook: 13-15 minutes

Make the shortbread cookies and fruit compotes a day ahead of serving, then assemble the stacks just before you need them. For a baby's christening or birthday, sprinkle the tops with pink or blue sugar confetti or tiny sugar shapes.

1 cup crème fraîche
or whipped cream

confectioners' sugar, sifted,
for dusting

SHORTBREAD

1¼ cups all-purpose flour, plus
extra for dusting

3 tablespoons cornstarch

¼ cup superfine or granulated
sugar, plus extra for sprinkling

finely grated rind of 1 lemon

1 stick unsalted butter, chilled
and diced

FRUIT COMPOTES

2 teaspoons cornstarch

¼ cup superfine or
granulated sugar

juice of 1 lemon

1 cup blueberries,
plus 12 to decorate

1 cup raspberries,
plus 12 to decorate

1. Preheat the oven to 325°F.

2. For the shortbread, put the flour, cornstarch, sugar, and lemon rind into a mixing bowl and stir together. Rub in the butter, using your fingertips, until the mixture resembles fine crumbs. Press together, using your hands, to make a ball of dough. Lightly dust a work surface with flour.

3. Knead the dough lightly, then cut it in half and roll out each half thinly. Stamp out 1¾-inch flower shapes or fluted circles, using a cookie cutter, and transfer to a nonstick baking sheet. Add the trimmings to the reserved dough and roll it out thinly, then stamp out more cookies and transfer them to another baking sheet. Continue until all the dough has been used; you should have at least 72 cookies. Sprinkle with extra sugar, then bake in the preheated oven for 8-10 minutes, or until pale golden. Let cool on the sheets.

4. To make the fruit compotes, divide the cornstarch, sugar, and lemon juice equally between 2 small, heavy saucepans. Add 1 cup of blueberries to the first pan and 1 cup of raspberries to the second. Gently heat both pans for 3-5 minutes, stirring, until the fruit has softened and the sauce thickened. Let cool, then stir.

5. When ready to serve, put a teaspoonful of crème fraîche on two-thirds of the cookies, top half of these with a teaspoon of raspberry compote (you may need to break up the raspberries first), press a cream-topped cookie on top, then add a teaspoonful of blueberry compote. Complete with a third cookie, then transfer to a serving plate. Top half the stacks with a raspberry and half with a blueberry and dust with sifted confectioners' sugar.

Mini Clementine sorbets

Makes: 10
Prep: 25 minutes
Cook: 5 minutes
Freeze: 4 hours plus overnight

If you are serving these only to adults, you might like to add a splash of Cointreau or Grand Marnier to the mixture before freezing.

10 Clementines

⅓ cup granulated sugar

¼ cup water

finely grated rind and juice of 1 lemon

juice of 1 large orange

1. Cut a thin slice off the top of each Clementine and set aside. Squeeze a little of the juice from each fruit into a blender. Using a teaspoon, scoop the flesh into the blender, then process to a puree.

2. Press the puree through a strainer into a large loaf pan. Put the 10 Clementine cups into a roasting pan and freeze.

3. Put the sugar and water into a heavy saucepan. Heat gently for 5 minutes, or until the sugar has dissolved, tilting the pan to mix them together. Increase the heat and boil rapidly without stirring for 1 minute. Remove from the heat, then stir in the lemon rind and juice. Pour the lemon syrup and orange juice through a strainer and onto the Clementine puree, stir, then let cool.

4. Transfer the loaf pan to the freezer and freeze for 2 hours, or until the mixture is semifrozen. Break up the ice crystals using a fork, then return to the freezer for 1 hour. Beat again with the fork, then freeze for an additional 1 hour. Beat again until it resembles colored snow.

5. Spoon the sorbet into the Clementine cups, add the lids at a slanted angle, and freeze overnight. (If the sorbet has frozen too firmly, let it soften at room temperature for a few minutes, then beat with a fork.) When ready to serve, transfer the iced desserts to a plate.

Striped cranberry and amaretti creams

Makes: 10
Prep: 30 minutes
Cook: 5-8 minutes
Chill: 1 hour

An easy festive dessert that makes a great alternative to the traditional Christmas treat. Children will love to help you make the sugar stars.

⅓ cup superfine or granulated sugar

2 teaspoons cornstarch

a large pinch of ground cinnamon

a large pinch of ground ginger

½ cup water

2 cups frozen cranberries

AMARETTI CREAM

⅔ cup cream cheese

3 tablespoons superfine or granulated sugar

1 cup heavy cream

4 teaspoons orange juice or Cointreau

12 amaretti cookies, crushed

SUGAR STARS

confectioners' sugar, for dusting

6 ounces ready-to-use fondant

1. Put the sugar, cornstarch, cinnamon, and ginger into a medium, heavy saucepan, then gradually mix in the water until smooth. Add the frozen cranberries and cook gently for 5-8 minutes, stirring from time to time, until they are soft and the compote has thickened. Cover and let cool.

2. For the amaretti cream, put the cream cheese and sugar into a mixing bowl and stir, then gradually whisk in the cream until smooth. Stir in the orange juice and then the cookie crumbs. Spoon the mixture into a paper or plastic disposable pastry bag. Spoon the cranberry compote into another disposable pastry bag. Snip off the tips.

3. Pipe amaretti cream into 10 shot glasses until they are one-quarter full. Pipe over half the cranberry compote, then repeat the layers. Cover and chill in the refrigerator for 1 hour.

4. For the sugar stars, line a baking sheet with nonstick parchment paper. Lightly dust a work surface with confectioners' sugar. Knead the fondant lightly, then roll it out thinly. Stamp out stars of different sizes, using tiny star cutters, then transfer to the prepared baking sheet and let harden at room temperature for 1 hour, or until needed. Arrange the stars on the desserts and around the bottoms of the glasses just before you serve them.

Chocolate and caramel cups

Makes: 12
Prep: 30 minutes
Cook: 7–8 minutes
Chill: 2 hours

If you don't have any petit four liners, line the cups of a mini muffin pan with small squares of plastic wrap, spread melted chocolate over the plastic wrap, then peel it away before serving.

6 ounces semisweet dark
chocolate, coarsely chopped

½ cup granulated sugar

¼ cup water

12 small walnut halves

2 tablespoons unsalted butter

½ cup heavy cream

1. Line a 12-cup mini muffin pan with paper petit four liners. Line a baking sheet with nonstick parchment paper.

2. Put the chocolate in a heatproof bowl, set the bowl over a saucepan of gently simmering water, and heat until melted. Put a spoonful of melted chocolate into each paper liner, then brush over the sides evenly using a small pastry brush. Chill for 30 minutes, then brush on a second layer of chocolate, being careful around the sides so there is an even thickness. Cover and chill in the refrigerator.

3. Put the sugar and water into a small, heavy saucepan. Heat gently for 5 minutes, or until the sugar has dissolved, tilting the pan to mix them together. Increase the heat and boil rapidly without stirring for 4–5 minutes, until the caramel is deep golden (see page 7). Remove from the heat, add the walnuts, quickly coat them in the caramel, then lift them out using 2 forks. Put them on the prepared baking sheet, slightly apart.

4. Add the butter to the remaining caramel, tilt the pan to mix, then gradually stir in the cream. Transfer to a bowl, let cool, then cover and chill in the refrigerator for 1½ hours, or until thick. Lift the chocolate-lined paper liners out of the pan. Spoon the caramel cream into a large pastry bag fitted with a large star tip and pipe it into the chocolate cups. Chill in the refrigerator until required. Decorate with the caramel walnuts just before serving.

Mini Party Treats

Cherry and honey layered dessert

Makes: 30
Prep: 25 minutes
Cook: 10 minutes
Freeze: 30 minutes
Chill: 5 hours

This two-tone dessert is made by setting the gelatin mold at an angle before adding the creamy layer for an eye-catching effect.

1 (10-ounce) package frozen pitted cherries

2 tablespoons superfine or granulated sugar

¾ cup water

4 teaspoons powdered gelatin

1 cup ricotta

finely grated rind of 1 lemon

3 tablespoons honey

⅔ cup heavy cream

1. Put the frozen cherries, sugar, and ½ cup water into a medium, heavy saucepan, bring to a boil, then reduce the heat and simmer, uncovered, for 5 minutes, until the cherries have softened.

2. Meanwhile, put the remaining water in a small heatproof bowl, then sprinkle the gelatin over the surface, making sure the powder is absorbed. Set aside for 5 minutes. Set the bowl of gelatin in a heavy saucepan of gently simmering water and heat for 5 minutes, stirring from time to time, until the gelatin is a clear liquid (see page 7).

3. Process the cherry mixture in a blender until pureed, then pour back into the heavy saucepan. Stir in 2½ tablespoons of the gelatin mixture, then let cool.

4. Divide the cherry mixture among six ⅔-cup loaf pans, prop them up in the freezer so that the gelatin sets at an angle, then freeze for 30 minutes, or until firm.

5. Meanwhile, put the ricotta, lemon rind, and honey into a mixing bowl and stir together. Pour the cream into a large mixing bowl and whisk until it forms soft swirls, then fold it into the ricotta mixture. Add the remaining gelatin mixture and stir gently, then cover and let stand at room temperature.

6. When the cherry mixture is semifrozen, spoon the ricotta over the top, level, then cover and chill in the refrigerator for 4 hours, or until set.

7. To invert, dip each mold in a dish of just-boiled water for 2 seconds, then lift it out of the water. Loosen the edges of each dessert with a blunt knife, then invert onto a plate, remove the pan, and clean up the edge of the dessert with a sharp knife, if needed. Return to the refrigerator for 1 hour, then slice each dessert into five and serve.

Honey and pistachio ice cream with poached figs

Makes: 10
Prep: 30–35 minutes
Cook: 10 minutes
Freeze: 1–7 hours

Refreshingly cool and summery, this Greek-inspired dessert can be made in advance and looks best served with small figs.

ICE CREAM

6 egg yolks

2 teaspoons cornstarch

⅓ cup honey

2 cups milk

1 cup Greek yogurt

2 teaspoons rosewater (optional)

½ cup coarsely chopped pistachio nuts

POACHED FIGS

⅔ cup red wine

¼ cup superfine or granulated sugar

1 cinnamon stick, halved

10 small figs

1. For the ice cream, put the egg yolks, cornstarch, and honey into a large mixing bowl. Put the milk into a medium, heavy saucepan, bring to a boil, then gradually whisk it into the yolks. Strain the mixture through a strainer back into the pan and cook over low heat, stirring, until thickened and smooth. Pour the custard into a clean bowl, cover the surface with parchment paper, and let cool.

2. Whisk the yogurt and rosewater, if using, into the custard. Pour the mixture into a chilled ice cream machine and churn for 15–20 minutes, until thick and creamy. Mix in the pistachio nuts and churn until stiff enough to scoop. If you don't have an ice cream machine, pour into a large nonstick loaf pan for 3–4 hours, until semifrozen. Beat in a food processor, then stir in the pistachio nuts, return to the loaf pan, and freeze for an additional 3 hours, or until firm.

3. Meanwhile, for the poached figs, put the wine, sugar, and cinnamon stick into a small, heavy saucepan and heat gently. Add the figs (they should fit snugly into the pan) and poach gently for 5 minutes. Let cool.

4. When ready to serve, take the ice cream out of the freezer and let it soften at room temperature for 5–10 minutes. Scoop into small dishes and add 2 fig halves and a little of the syrup. Serve immediately.

Spiced plum spirals

Makes: 32
Prep: 30 minutes
Cook: 12–15 minutes

There's no need to make your own pastry for these. Simply unroll ready-to-use puff pastry, sprinkle with spiced sugar and orange, then roll up, slice, and bake. For this recipe, they are sandwiched with a spiced plum filling.

a little sunflower oil, for greasing

½ cup superfine or granulated sugar

1 teaspoon ground cinnamon

finely grated rind of 1 orange

2 ready-to-use puff pastry sheets

milk, for brushing

confectioners' sugar, sifted, for dusting

FILLING

5 plums, pitted and finely chopped

¼ cup superfine or granulated sugar

a large pinch of ground cinnamon

3 tablespoons water

1 teaspoon cornstarch

1. Preheat the oven to 400°F. Lightly brush 2 baking sheets with oil.

2. Put the sugar, cinnamon, and orange rind into a mixing bowl and stir.

3. Unroll a pastry sheet, roll it out if necessary, then cut it in half to make two 10 x 7½-inch pieces. Sprinkle both pieces with half the sugar mixture, then roll them up, starting with a long edge, and brush a little milk onto the ends to stick them in place. Cut each roll into 16 slices, then put the slices, cut side up, on one of the prepared baking sheets.

4. Repeat step 3 with the second pastry sheet. Bake all the pastry rolls in the preheated oven for 12–15 minutes, until golden.

5. Meanwhile, for the filling, put the plums into a heavy saucepan and add the sugar, cinnamon, and 2 tablespoons of water. Cover with a lid and cook over gentle heat for 10 minutes. Mix the cornstarch with the remaining 1 tablespoon of water in a small bowl, then stir it into the plums and cook for an additional minute, until thickened. Let cool.

6. Put a spoonful of the plum filling onto half the pastries, then top each with another pastry. Arrange on a serving plate and dust with confectioners' sugar.

Blueberry vodka gelatins

Makes: 12
Prep: 15 minutes
Cook: 8 minutes
Chill: 4 hours

This pretty dessert can be prepared in minutes. It looks stylish served in glasses of different heights, then arranged on individual dessert plates or saucers and sprinkled with pink edible glitter.

6 ladyfingers or thin slices of store-bought pound cake

1½ cups water

1 tablespoon powdered gelatin

2 cups blueberries

⅓ cup superfine or granulated sugar

finely grated rind of 1 lemon

½ cup vodka

½ cup heavy cream

pink edible glitter, to decorate

1. Cut out 12 small circles of cake, using the top of a liqueur glass as a guide, then press each of them into the bottom of a liqueur glass.

2. Put ¼ cup of water into a small bowl, then sprinkle the gelatin over the surface, making sure the powder is absorbed. Set aside for 5 minutes.

3. Meanwhile, put the blueberries, sugar, lemon rind, and remaining 1¼ cups of water into a heavy saucepan and bring to a boil, then reduce the heat and simmer, uncovered, for 5 minutes, until the fruit has softened.

4. Take the pan off the heat, add the gelatin, and stir until it has dissolved. Add the vodka, then pour the mixture into the glasses, pressing down the cake circles with a teaspoon if they begin to float. Let cool, then cover and put the glasses on a small baking sheet. Chill in the refrigerator for 4 hours, or until set.

5. When ready to serve, spoon 2 teaspoons of the cream over the top of each dessert, then sprinkle with pink edible glitter.

Iced chocolate and peppermint mousses

Makes: 12
Prep: 40 minutes
Cook: 10 minutes
Freeze: 4 hours

A classic French dessert with a twist. Because these little mousses are frozen, they can be made well in advance of your party. The drizzled chocolate decoration can be prepared the night before and kept in the refrigerator until you are ready to serve.

6 ounces semisweet dark chocolate, coarsely chopped

1 tablespoon unsalted butter, diced

3 eggs, separated

2 tablespoons milk

1 tablespoon superfine or granulated sugar

½ teaspoon peppermint extract

DECORATION

2 ounces semisweet dark chocolate, coarsely chopped

2 ounces white chocolate, coarsely chopped

a few drops of green food coloring

½ cup heavy cream

½–1 teaspoon peppermint extract

1. For the mousse, put the dark chocolate and butter in a heatproof bowl, set the bowl over a saucepan of gently simmering water, and heat until melted. Stir in the egg yolks, one at a time, then stir in the milk until smooth. Remove from the heat.

2. Whisk the egg whites in a large, clean mixing bowl until you have soft peaks. Gradually whisk in the sugar a teaspoonful at a time. Fold the egg whites into the melted chocolate mixture, then fold in the peppermint.

3. Spoon the mousse into 12 plastic shot glasses (if you have a funnel or large piping tip, spoon the mousse into this and pipe it into the glasses so that the sides don't get messy). Freeze for 4 hours, or overnight.

4. Meanwhile, for the decoration, line a baking sheet with nonstick parchment paper. Put the dark chocolate in a heatproof bowl, set the bowl over a saucepan of gently simmering water, and heat until melted. Drizzle spoonfuls of the melted chocolate over the prepared baking sheet in random squiggles, then chill in the refrigerator for 30 minutes.

5. Put the white chocolate for the decoration in a heatproof bowl, set the bowl over a saucepan of gently simmering water, and heat until melted. Drizzle half the melted white chocolate over the dark chocolate on the baking sheet. Stir the green food coloring into the remaining white chocolate and drizzle this over the other 2 layers of chocolate. Chill in the refrigerator for 30 minutes.

6. To decorate the mousses, pour the cream into a large bowl and whisk until it forms soft swirls, then stir in the peppermint extract. Spoon this onto the frozen desserts, then break the drizzled chocolate into pieces and press it into the cream. Let the desserts stand at room temperature for 10 minutes, then serve.

Tropical caramel custards

Makes: 10
Prep: 25 minutes
Cook: 30–35 minutes
Chill: 4 hours

Here's a dessert with an exotic twist, with the addition of orange, lime, and mango. If you don't have small metal molds, use little foil muffin or tart liners, but make sure they're 1½ inches deep.

¾ cup granulated sugar

¾ cup water

3 tablespoons boiling water

2 eggs, plus 2 egg yolks

⅔ cup low-fat milk

1 (14-ounce) can sweetened condensed milk

finely grated rind of 1 orange

finely grated rind of 1 lime

½ small mango, peeled and pitted, to decorate

1. Preheat the oven to 325°F. Put ten ⅔-cup individual metal molds or dariole molds in a roasting pan.

2. Put the sugar and water into a heavy saucepan. Heat gently for 5 minutes, or until the sugar has dissolved, tilting the pan to mix them together. Increase the heat and boil rapidly without stirring for 5 minutes, until the caramel is deep golden (see page 7). Remove from the heat and add the boiling water, but stand well back because the syrup will spit. Let the syrup cool for 1 minute, or until the bubbles begin to subside, then divide it among the molds.

3. Put the eggs and egg yolks into a medium bowl, then whisk lightly with a fork.

4. Pour the milk and condensed milk into a heavy saucepan. Bring just to a boil over low heat, stirring constantly. Slowly pour this into the egg yolks, then strain it back into the pan. Stir in the orange rind and half the lime rind (wrap the rest in plastic wrap and reserve).

5. Pour the custard into the molds. Pour warm water into the roasting pan to come halfway up the sides of the molds. Bake in the preheated oven for 20–25 minutes, or until the custard is set. Lift the molds out of the water, let them cool, then chill in the refrigerator for 4 hours, or overnight.

6. To serve, cut the mango into small, thin slices. Dip each mold in a dish of just-boiled water for 10 seconds, then lift it out of the water. Loosen the edges of each dessert with a blunt knife, then invert them onto a plate and remove the mold. Serve topped with the mango slices and sprinkled with the reserved lime rind.

Mini chocolate éclairs with Irish cream

Makes: 36
Prep: 45 minutes
Cook: 20–25 minutes
Set: 15 minutes

A great crowd-pleaser, but if serving to a gathering of mixed ages, divide the cream and add just 2 tablespoons of Irish cream liqueur to half of it, serving the liqueur-free version to the children.

4 tablespoons unsalted butter, plus extra for greasing

⅔ cup water

½ cup all-purpose flour

a pinch of salt

2 eggs, beaten

a few drops of vanilla extract

FILLING

1½ cups heavy cream

2 tablespoons confectioners' sugar, sifted

¼ cup Irish cream liqueur

TOPPING

2 tablespoons unsalted butter, diced

4 ounces semisweet dark chocolate, coarsely chopped

1 tablespoon confectioners' sugar, sifted

2 teaspoons milk

1. Preheat the oven to 400°F. Lightly grease 2 baking sheets with butter.

2. Put the butter and water into a medium, heavy saucepan and heat gently until the butter has melted. Increase the heat and bring to a boil, then remove from the heat. Sift in the flour and salt, then return the pan to the heat and stir together until the mixture makes a smooth ball that leaves the sides of the pan clean. Let cool for at least 15 minutes.

3. Gradually beat in the eggs, beating well after each addition, until the mixture is smooth. Stir in the vanilla. Spoon the mixture into a large pastry bag fitted with a ½-inch plain piping tip, then pipe 1½-inch long éclairs onto the prepared baking sheets.

4. Bake in the preheated oven for 10–12 minutes, until well risen and crisp on the outside. Make a slit in the side of each éclair to let the steam escape, then put them back in the oven for 2 minutes. Let cool.

5. About 1 hour before serving, make the filling. Pour the cream into a large mixing bowl, add the sifted confectioners' sugar and cream liqueur, and whisk until it forms soft swirls. Spoon this into a pastry bag fitted with a star tip, then pipe it into the éclairs.

6. For the topping, put all the ingredients in a heatproof bowl, set the bowl over a saucepan of gently simmering water, and heat until melted, smooth, and glossy, stirring once or twice. Spoon this over the éclairs, let set for 15 minutes, then transfer to a serving plate.

Coffee parfait bites

Makes: 20
Prep: 30 minutes
Cook: 12–15 minutes
Set: 1½ hours

Bite through the crisp coffee macaron into the creamy, smooth coffee parfait filling. If you serve these in pretty paper liners, you won't need to give your guests plates.

1⅓ cups confectioners' sugar

⅓ cup firmly packed
light brown sugar

1¼ cups almond meal
(ground almonds)

3 extra-large egg whites

4 ounces semisweet dark
chocolate, coarsely chopped,
to decorate

PARFAIT

¼ cup granulated sugar

3 tablespoons water

2 egg yolks

2 teaspoons instant coffee
granules

1 stick unsalted butter, softened
and diced

1. Line 3 baking sheets with nonstick parchment paper. Put the confectioners' sugar, light brown sugar, and almond meal into a food processor and process until finely ground, then press through a strainer into a mixing bowl and set aside.

2. Whisk the egg whites in a large, clean mixing bowl until you have soft peaks. Gently fold half the almond mixture into the eggs, using a large spoon, then fold in the remaining mixture until you have a smooth, soft mixture that falls gently from the spoon.

3. Spoon the mixture into a pastry bag fitted with a large, plain tip and pipe circles about 1 inch in diameter onto the paper, leaving a little space between them. Let stand for 10–15 minutes to dry. Preheat the oven to 325°F.

4. Bake the macarons in the preheated oven for 12–15 minutes, or until they can be lifted off the paper, then let cool.

5. For the parfait, put the granulated sugar and water into a heavy saucepan. Heat gently for 4–5 minutes, until the sugar has dissolved, tilting the pan to mix them together. Increase the heat and boil rapidly without stirring until the temperature reaches 225°F on a candy thermometer, or until there is a hint of color around the edges.

6. Meanwhile, put the egg yolks into a mixing bowl, then whisk in the coffee. As soon as the syrup is ready, gradually whisk it into the yolks in a thin trickle until the mixture is thick and cool, then whisk in the butter piece by piece. Cover and let cool, then sandwich together the macarons in pairs with the parfait.

7. For the decoration, put the chocolate in a heatproof bowl, set the bowl over a saucepan of gently simmering water, and heat until melted. Put the melted chocolate into a paper pastry bag and snip off the tip, then pipe zigzag lines over the top of the macarons. Let stand in a cool place for the chocolate to harden, then serve.

Index